Frontier Family Life

Frontier Family Life

A PHOTOGRAPHIC CHRONICLE OF THE OLD WEST

MARIANNE BELL

BARNES
&NOBLE
BOOKS
NEW YORK

This edition published by Barnes and Noble, Inc., by
arrangement with Saraband Inc.

1998 Barnes & Noble Books

Copyright © 1998 Saraband Inc.

Design © Ziga Design

10 9 8 7 6 5 4 3 2

Library of Congress Cataloging in Publication Data available

ISBN: 0-7607-1103-8

Printed in China

— FOR JUDY

Contents

~ Introduction   6

~ Beyond the Frontier   12

~ With Hope in Their Hearts   32

~ A Promised Land   54

~ O Pioneers!   70

~ Our Town   100

~ Index   111

~ Bibliography & Acknowledgements   112

Introduction

What were the dreams that impelled men and women to hazard great dangers and hardships to seek a new home in the Far West during the nineteenth century? By 1800 the land east of the Mississippi was rapidly filling up with migrants to the first great American West—beyond the Appalachian Mountains. They had followed the Wilderness Road blazed by Daniel Boone through the Cumberland Gap in 1769 and formed new settlements in Kentucky, western Virginia, Tennessee and the Ohio River Valley.

Far-ranging trappers and traders pushed into new territory, returning with tales of fortunes to be made in gold, furs, land and other natural resources. Enthusiastic explorers and pioneers encouraged migration to the areas they had opened to Anglo settlement: Stephen Austin in Texas, Jason Lee in Oregon, Jedediah Smith, who found the South Pass that provided a route for wagons across the Rocky Mountains. Popular culture glorified the doctrine of Manifest Destiny and painted vivid pictures of a frontier experience that was larger than life, from James Fenimore Cooper's Natty Bumppo to nineteenth-century dime novels, captivity stories, Wild West shows and romantic Currier & Ives prints of an idyllic West dotted with scenic wonders and "noble savages."

As historian Alvin M. Josephy, Jr., points out in his introduction to *The World Almanac of the American West* (Pharos Books, 1986): "We have long known the stock image of the hardy frontiersman. But what of the roles and trials of the equally hardy frontier women who were with him, and of the blacks and other minorities who also populated the West?" The following pages aim to present a more balanced and representative "family album" of life across the full spectrum of the frontier than those treatments that focus on outsized heroes and villains engaged in endless warfare with the environment and one another. In the words of historian Susan Armitage, "Even the most heroic people lead ordinary lives 99 percent of the time...." Thus, "ordinary lives are the true story of the West, for men as well as for women." The photographs gathered here offer a glimpse into the daily chores, humble homes, makeshift household solutions and recreational activities that comprised family life on the frontier.

The Frontier Thesis proposed by historian Frederick Jackson Turner in 1893 identified a series of frontiers that interacted dynamically to imprint the national character and the course of American history. These frontiers—of the trader, the miner, the farmer and the rancher—form a context in which to explore everyday pioneer life, with its various tasks, tribulations and enjoyments. Whether they traveled west by wagon train, stagecoach, steamer, or railroad, "the movers," as they were called, faced similar difficulties, not only on the way, but upon arrival.

Those who settled the Great Plains had to improvise shelter from "bricks" of sod, or make dugouts with turf façades, as there was little wood or stone for building. Streams were scarce, and wells had to be dug to pump water for household use and livestock. Extremes of weather

Opposite: Mormon immigrants at Needles Rock, Utah, their path marked by newly erected telegraph poles.

Page 1 photograph: A moment of comradeship.

Page 2: The Ira Watson family of Sargent, Nebraska, in 1886.

Page 4: Pioneer sisters with their children atop the great pile of stones unearthed in clearing the fields.

Above: *Mounted scouts escort a long wagon train on the Great Plains.*

Opposite: *A hopeful prospector sluices a California stream for gold.*

included blizzards, torrential rains, wind storms, even tornadoes, while summer's heat was relentless, unrelieved by the breezes of coastal regions. Families arrived with little or no livestock, apart from the oxen that pulled their wagon trains, so farm animals had to be bred or purchased on the spot—milk cows, hunting dogs, poultry, pigs, horses and mules.

Settlers of the Southwest included many Mexicans, whose Spanish conquerors had long controlled present-day Arizona, New Mexico and California, after wresting the land from native peoples on both sides of the Rio Grande. Later, Anglo settlers added a new factor to the

equation. Both the nomadic Apache and the settled Pueblo dwellers suffered from the clash of cultures in this multiethnic region, just as the buffalo hunting tribes of the Great Plains would resist the incursions of farmers and ranchers. Over time, newcomers adopted regional styles in adobe housing, livestock tending, cooking and food preservation. Cowboys learned their skills from the hard-riding Mexican *vaqueros*, with their lariats and chaparajos (anglicized to "chaps"—leather leggings worn to protect the rider's legs from thorny underbrush). The Cattle Kingdom would come into its own after completion of the transcontinental railroad in 1869, when thousands of head of half-wild livestock were rounded up for trail drives to railheads like Abilene and Dodge City, Kansas, from which beef was shipped East.

In California, the Spanish colonial era gave way before the influx of prospectors who streamed to the West Coast during the gold rush that began in 1849, after the discovery of gold in the American River, near present-day Sacramento. Only the year before, Mexico had ceded California to the United States in the wake of the Mexican War. Originally, the region drew thousands of transients in the grip of gold fever, but few of them found the riches they had sought. Instead, they turned to farming and ranching, making "the Golden State" a byword for productive agriculture. The native tribes that had resisted domination by Mexico moved ever deeper into the hills to avoid contact with the new intruders, but they were largely displaced, or pressed into service as cheap laborers for the mines and farms.

After 1859 the discovery of the rich Comstock Lode drew some 20,000 prospectors and miners into the newly created Nevada Territory. Rough mining camps like Goldhill, Silverton and Leadville sprang up in the future

Rocky Mountain States and the Sierra Nevada. The solitary prospector panning for gold was soon replaced by cadres of miners extracting precious metals from veins deep in the earth. "Mail-order brides" from the East arrived to lend a sense of order and gentility, as the mining camps evolved into permanent communities. Many of these settlements would become ghost towns after the mines were "played out," but fortunes were made and lost in the meantime, and people staked their futures on the turn of a card. The mining frontier would become a part of national folklore as far north as the Klondike, where new bonanzas in the late 1890s saw both male and female prospectors trekking into the wilderness to create yet another cycle of boom and bust. As before, many of those who found no gold struck new roots as merchants, farmers and laborers.

Western cities like San Francisco, Denver and Santa Fe burgeoned into major centers of commerce and industry. The Mormon settlers of Utah made Salt Lake City, their New Zion, the center of a vast agricultural and spiritual enterprise in the arid Great Basin. Freedmen and women born into slavery came west after the Civil War to establish a new way of life. Omaha, Nebraska, prospered as a railway center, and Cheyenne, Wyoming, became a hub of the ranching industry and pushed for territorial status. It also led the nation in granting woman suffrage, in 1869, and in having the first woman governor— Nellie Tayloe Ross.

On the local level, countless pioneer women were instrumental in shaping their communities, from schools and churches to libraries and cultural activites. They also took active roles in such issues as temperance and the relief of indigent minorities, while carrying out the never-ending duties of child rearing, homemaking, and laborious chores that ranged from splitting logs to branding cattle. Others

became colorful characters as frontier madams, sharp-shooters, stunt riders, outlaws and dance-hall entertainers.

Couples who formed mixed marriages, including Anglo-Indian and Hispanic families, often faced rejection from both sides of the bloodline. And Chinese immigrants of both sexes were long confined to hard labor at low wages, or, in the case of young women, to prostitution, when promises of domestic labor or marriage did not materialize. It would be many years before immigrants from the Orient could become naturalized citizens, with at least nominal protection of their civil rights.

Despite the great diversity of people and circumstances on the frontier, the nineteenth-century pioneers all shared one common experience: change. Shelter, food and water were their first priorities, and these were closely followed by issues relating to family health and basic safety. Many of the settlers had taken such necessities for granted before they undertook frontier life. Isolation, too, was a shock to most of those who settled remote ranches and homesteads. "This had truly been the longest and most dreary week of my life, and the first one without seeing and talking with those of my own sex," complained Annie Green, upon moving with her husband to a ranch near Greeley, Colorado. Conversely, those who moved to newly founded towns sometimes found the "rough justice" and colorful characters they encountered difficult to adjust to, and sincerely wished for a more "civilized," or quieter, environment. For the Native Americans who were displaced, the change in lifeways was radical: large numbers did not survive.

Frontier life was not, however, always a battle against harsh weather, hunger, violent intruders and ill health, any more than it resembled the popular myths of the overnight rush to fortune or the glamorous, carefree existence of the freewheeling cowboy. Among the daily trials

and tribulations, there was pride in the establishment of a functional home, however rudimentary; opportunity was abundant; hopes and dreams were plentiful. The pictorial history that follows is a tribute to the men, women and children who took up the challenge of carving out a new life in a vast area that had been *terra incognita* to all but its native peoples. Whether they came from the Eastern Seaboard, the newly settled Midwest, "south of the border," or lands beyond the seas, each pioneer family left its imprint on the dynamic, ever-receding Western frontier.

Opposite: *Class picture from a one-room schoolhouse, where patriotism and piety were included in the curriculum.*

Below: *The flourishing Hohman family of Custer County, Nebraska.*

Beyond the Frontier

Long before the nineteenth-century waves of immigration from the East Coast to the unknown reaches of the trans-Mississippi West, many families and communities had been established there, whether in tribal or other ethnic groups, or as isolated enclaves formed by Christian missionaries, military outposts, or mixed marriages among various peoples.

For Hispanic families from Mexico, what is now the American Southwest was *El Norte*—the northern frontier of their homeland. In 1598 the Spanish government had sent Don Juan de Oñate from northern Mexico into the Texas and New Mexico area to establish a colony. Spanish missionaries and settlers soon came into conflict with the Native Americans of Acoma Pueblo (founded about AD 1150), which resulted in the destruction of North America's oldest continuously inhabited community. Soon afterward, Oñate and other explorers sent out by Spain established claims on the West Coast from the Gulf of California to Oregon. As a result, new missionaries and colonists settled parts of this huge region, as they had done in the lands beyond the Rio Grande—now Texas, New Mexico and Arizona. Mexican immigrants to California encountered less resistance than the Pueblo peoples had offered. The tribes of this area were primarily nomadic hunter-gatherers, some of whom were converted to Christianity by Franciscan missionaries, while others melted into the hills and avoided contact with the intruders.

Native Americans of the Northwest, Great Basin and Great Plains regions were relatively free of interference with their ways of life from non-native immigrants until the early nineteenth century. They traded intermittently with French-Canadians and Americans, and sometimes intermarried with them, as did members of the Hispanic and Pueblo communities of the Southwest. However, families formed by these mixed marriages were often ostracized as "half-breeds" by ethnic groups on both sides of the bloodline.

The U.S. Army had little involvement in the West until the Mexican War of 1846-48, in which the United States acquired vast new territories in the Southwest and present-day California. Meanwhile, the military presence had begun to grow on grounds of protecting the increasing numbers of settlers from hostile native peoples, and, in turn, safeguarding the Native Americans from exploitation and mistreatment—with very mixed results. Additional forts sprang up in the late 1860s, many of them commanded by Civil War veterans like General George A. Custer. Officers' wives and families accompanied them on assignments to forts all over the Great Plains and the Southwest. By this time, pressure from incoming tribes displaced from Eastern homelands, and from the waves of migration inspired by the gold and silver rushes and facilitated by the new transcontinental railroad, had made the Far West a volatile region widely affected by culture shock. However, both indigenous and new families and communities sought to pursue their ways of life in relative peace and dignity, adapting themselves to changing times as best they could.

Opposite: A descendant of the original Southwestern peoples – the cliff dwellers known as the Anasazi, or Old Ones. They built adobe complexes in the sheltering walls of steep cliffs like Colorado's Mesa Verde and farmed communal fields below. Today's Pueblo peoples share a cultural heritage more than a thousand years old.

SOUTHWESTERN NATIVE AMERICA

Opposite: Ladders reach to the upper levels of an adobe "apartment house" facing onto a common courtyard, where Hopi women clean corn. *Left:* Chiles are strung for drying at New Mexico's San Ildefonso Pueblo. *Below, left:* Hopi girls weave baskets with intricate designs for food storage at Shipaulovi, Arizona. Their traditional squash-blossom hairstyle shows that they are of marriageable age. *Below:* Ancient cliff dwellings in the rock walls of Canyon de Chelly, Arizona. Other traces of the Anasazi have been found in the Cave of Life in Arizona's Petrified Forest. The artefacts include petroglyphs, shell jewelry, prehistoric stone carvings and fragments of pottery bearing natural motifs still used by Southwestern tribes today.

ON THE PLAINS

Opposite: Edward S. Curtis's 1900 portrait of three Piegan warriors on the vanishing Great Plains. *Right:* Oglala Sioux in Wyoming conduct funeral rites for their chief's daughter, whose body is exposed above ground according to Plains custom. *Below right:* Arapaho women cure deerskin to be used as clothing and bedding. *Below:* A Kiowa infant in the traditional cradleboard, which was carried on the mother's back or propped nearby while she was working.

NORTHERN NATIVE AMERICA

Left: A child of the Canadian subarctic, warmly dressed in fur and hide garments and equipped with snowshoes. *Below, left:* A nomadic Inuit family at their summer camp, with dwellings made of caribou hide stretched over driftwood poles. *Below:* For a Qagyuhl clan wedding, the bride brought a dowry of slaves and luxury goods to be passed on to her children (Edward S. Curtis photograph).

Opposite: An Ojibwa woman and child gather wild rice on Saskatchewan's Garson Lake. Originally, members of this tribe lived in the Eastern Woodlands region, but they were pushed west by successive waves of native and Anglo migration.

HISPANIC COMMUNITIES

Opposite: Emigrants from Mexico shared cultural roots with Southwestern native peoples. In this turn-of-the-century photograph, a family transplanted to New Mexico husks corn, their staple food, for drying and storage. *Right:* Baking bread in the traditional horno, a beehive-shaped oven made of adobe, or sun-dried clay. This building material was common to Southwestern natives and Spanish settlers, who imported it to the New World from the Mediterranean region.

SPANISH COLONIAL INFLUENCE

Left: Spanish colonization of the Southwest from Mexico began in 1598 and continued long after Mexico declared its independence from Spain in 1821. By that time, most Mexicans had mixed native and European ancestry, like these ranchers photographed in New Mexico's Mora Valley in 1895.

Opposite: Mexican converts to Christianity imported their faith north of the border, as seen in this simple adobe church dating to the turn of the century. *Below: Haciendas* served by well water, and watering troughs made of hollow tree trunks, were a familiar sight in Santa Fe well into the twentieth century.

THE MISSIONARY FRONTIER

All of North America was once considered "mission territory" by Europeans who introduced their ways to native peoples in good faith, but too often with dismal results. On the opposite page, Roman Catholic missionaries at St. Joseph's School in British Columbia teach native children to knit and sew. At right, Presbyterian missionaries visit an aged Apache woman at Anadarko, Oklahoma Territory. Below, a mission school for Seminole children and adolescents. The Seminoles were forcibly removed from their Southeastern lands during the 1830s, except for those who took refuge in remote places like the Florida Everglades.

INTERETHNIC MARRIAGES

People living on the frontier were freer to contract mixed marriages than those along the Atlantic Seaboard, although they might still face hostility and even ostracism. *Opposite:* An Idaho mountain man with his Indian wife and their children. *Below:* An Anglo-Indian couple married *a la façon du pays*—according to the custom of the country. *Below, right:* An officer of the law and his family in southern California.

ARMY FAMILIES

Opposite: Roughing it at a 10th Cavalry camp near Chloride, New Mexico, in 1892. Patrolling the border with Mexico was a hazardous job, thanks to raiding parties, cattle rustlers and gangs like the notorious Cowboys. *Right:* A May Day picnic for army families among the chapparal and saguaro cactus of Arizona's Fort McDowell. *Below:* Officers and their wives at George A. Custer's 7th Cavalry camp at Big Timber, Kansas, five years after the Civil War ended.

OFF DUTY

Opposite: Troop L's baseball team and mascot posed for this portrait at 9th Cavalry headquarters in Fort Wingate, New Mexico, in 1899. Most of the original frontier cavalrymen were Civil War veterans, but recruitment expanded the ranks of soldiers trained for duty in the Far West. *Right:* The 9th Cavalry band performs at the plaza in Santa Fe, New Mexico, photographed by Ben Wittick in 1880.

With Hope in Their Hearts

Since 1893 the standard framework for viewing the westward expansion of the United States has been the Frontier Thesis proposed by historian Frederick Jackson Turner. His bold interpretation of national history moved its focus from Eastern institutions imported from the Old World to the dynamic interplay of forces created by "the existence of an area of free land, its continuous recession, and the advance of American settlement westward." This chapter explores the experiences of men and women who journeyed to settle some of the successive frontiers identified by Turner, which included those of the trader, the rancher, the miner and the farmer, each of whom blazed a trail for the next wave of migrants.

As Eastern land became more crowded and expensive into the early nineteenth century, restless and disaffected Americans took advantage of the opportunities created by new or improved forms of transportation to move onward. The covered Conestoga wagon, or "prairie schooner," first built by German immigrants to Pennsylvania, was enlarged to carry loads of several tons and formed into wagon trains for the protection of travelers to cheap, plentiful government lands west of the Mississippi. Both the Santa Fe and Oregon Trails were opened between 1825 and 1830, when St. Louis, Missouri, became identified as "the gateway to the West." A network of national railroads was extended to California with completion of the Union Pacific line in 1869. Meanwhile, road and canal building, stagecoach travel and steamboats that plied the Mississippi and its tributaries provided new access to the Far West. Whatever the means by which the pioneers traveled, and irrespective of their destinations, each would discover that life on the trail was an adventure in itself.

The discovery of gold at Sutter's Mill, California, in 1848 opened up a miners' frontier that brought hordes of prospectors with dreams of striking it rich, not only to the Golden State, as it would be nicknamed, but to far-flung shanty towns and miners' camps in other territories and as far north as the Canadian Klondike. A rich vein of gold and silver, called the "Big Bonanza," was discovered near Virginia City, Nevada Territory, in 1873. It would produce a fortune estimated between $150 million and $200 million. Other valuable minerals, including copper, would foster a prosperous mining industry that provided employment, if not riches, to thousands who took the westward trail. Other settlers became merchants who supplied the needs of the mining communities.

Both social and economic factors contributed heavily to post-Civil War migration, especially by impoverished Southerners from the defeated Confederacy and newly freed African Americans who had been born into slavery. For the first time, they saw the opportunity to own land and enter trades and professions formerly closed to them and their offspring. These courageous freedmen and freedwomen, along with Northern blacks who rejected the endemic racism they had experienced, would make major contributions to the settlement and development of the American West.

Opposite: The founders of the Shores family, seen here in 1887, went west after the Civil War to start a new life on the Nebraska plains. Like most former slaves, they took the surname of their previous owners.

THE PRAIRIE SCHOONERS

Above and opposite: Use of the covered wagon, originated by eighteenth-century German immigrants to Pennsylvania, became widespread as large trains were formed for westward migration during the 1800s. Teams of oxen, which would be used for plowing and hauling after the journey, provided slow but steady progress.

No. 2853. "The Deadwood Coach."
Photo. and copyright by Grabill, '89.

REALITY AND IDEAL

Opposite: The Deadwood Coach makes its precarious way over a crude trestle bridge in *South Dakota*. The comparatively fast horse-drawn stagecoach was a desperately uncomfortable means of transport. It traveled some 2,000 miles of dusty or muddy Western roads on the famous "oxbow" route between Tipton, *Missouri*, and *San Francisco*. *Below:* Idealized images of beautiful scenery and "noble savages" fueled the drive to make the grueling journey to the *Far West*, in constant danger from hostile *Native* raiding parties, brutal heat and cold and nearly impassable mountains.

HALTS ON THE WAY

Left: The Conestoga became a "chuckwagon" when the backboard was lowered onto folding supports for cooking on the trail, as seen here in New Mexico. *Below:* A crowded camp in Nebraska, with typical log-and-frame shelters and livestock enclosures. *Opposite:* Making camp on a journey through Navajo country, in present-day New Mexico, during the 1890s. *Inset:* A wagon bogs down in the mud of the Weber River near Ogden, Utah.

BY RAIL AND BY WATERWAY

Left: Jubilant passengers pose on the first train to cross the Allegheny Mountains—a milestone in opening the West to settlement. The first printed suggestion for a transcontinental railroad appeared in *The Emigrant,* published in Ann Arbor, Michigan, in 1832. *Opposite:* Steamships that plied the Mississippi and its tributaries, the Ohio and the Missouri, played a major role in transportation. This steamer, named for South Dakota's Fort Pierre (formerly Fort Tecumseh), was photographed on the Missouri, the nation's longest river.

THE PROSPECTORS—
GETTING THERE

Opposite: Hell-bent on finding gold in Alaska's streambeds, placer miners climb the arduous Chilkoot Pass during the Klondike gold rush of the late 1890s. *Inset:* Both Alaska and British Columbia offered formidable obstacles to would-be miners during the nineteenth-century stampede into the wilderness in search of valuable minerals. *Below:* Pack trains of hardy, sure-footed burros were essential to prospectors from the Rocky Mountains to the Alaska Range.

EQUAL OPPORTUNITY

Some adventurous women broke ground on the mining frontier, as seen in the picture on the opposite page, taken in Idaho; the inset shows prospectors of the California gold rush. The miners—some with their wives—moved eastward after gold was found at Pike's Peak, Colorado, in 1859 (right). The days of the lone prospector (below) were numbered: mining's future would pass to capitalists who could finance the equipment needed to extract gold from quartz deposits deep below the surface.

REMOTE CABINS AND CAMPS

Journalist Bret Harte raised awareness of the mining
frontier with stories like "The Luck of Roaring Camp,"
and cartoons (inset) dramatized the plight of the lonely miner.
In the picture above, music-hall entertainers cross the icy
Dyea River en route to a Klondike mining settlement.

"SEEING THE ELEPHANT"

In Yukon Territory, women prospectors (inset) join the throngs who left from rugged jumping-off places like Dyea Point (main picture) to join the Klondike gold rush in hopes of "seeing the elephant"—the elusive mineral wealth of the mining frontiers.

FREEDOM SEEKERS

The prospect of independence brought thousands of African Americans across the Mississippi in the decades after the Civil War. Among those who braved the hardships were Colorado pioneers, at left, William Johnson, Ira Melton and Laura Bell, holding a promising litter of puppies from their hunting dogs. On the opposite page, Kansas settlers included the John Summer family of Dunlap (top left) and homesteaders to the former Indian Territory (top right) near present-day Guthrie, Oklahoma. Below are members of the Moses Speese family, photographed on their flourishing farm in Custer County, Nebraska, in 1888.

IN THEIR OWN RIGHT

Opposite, far left: Primus Biffle emigrated to Pueblo, Colorado, in 1891, and worked as a mason until he lost an arm to tuberculosis of the bone. After his recovery, he was employed as a porter by the Colorado Fuel and Iron Company hospital. *Near left:* Homesteader Edward Hannah, foreground, and two helpers make hay in Nebraska's Sand Hills country.

Left: An unidentified Texan at her spinning wheel; *Right:* midwife Sybil Harbor of Oregon; *Above:* journalist and activist Elizabeth W. Seymour of Colorado; *Top:* Denver's Clara Brown, who used her earnings as a laundress to help other former slaves emigrate to the Rocky Mountain region.

NEW FAMILIES, NEW FUTURES

Opposite: A young family poses in front of their sturdy board house with sash windows in Kansas, which became a state in 1861. *This page:* At right, Mrs. George Jenkins of Clark County, Kansas, and her children take care of their animals. Below, handsome Nebraska newlyweds pose for their wedding picture. At left, a Colorado boy in his Sunday best wears the solemn look demanded by nineteenth-century portrait photographers.

A Promised Land

Among those who immigrated to the West during the nineteenth century were both Americans and Europeans who fled religious persecution, poverty, or civil unrest in their original homes. The largest internal migration undertaken for religious reasons was that of the Mormons—members of the Church of Jesus Christ of Latter-Day Saints. Founded in 1830 at Fayette, New York, by Joseph Smith and thirty followers, the Saints, as they called themselves, were soon driven from the area by established religions and eventually made their way to Nauvoo, Illinois (1841), where they hoped to settle and build a temple.

In 1844 a riot broke out around the Mormon teaching of polygamy: Joseph Smith was killed, and Brigham Young was chosen as the new leader and prophet. He led the Mormons from Nauvoo to the arid Great Basin, where they established their Zion at the Great Salt Lake. Thousands of Mormon settlers and converts soon came to the new capital, some from the East Coast, others from Europe. They organized irrigation systems, divided the land according to need and capability, and established new settlements both in and out of the territory that they called Deseret (present-day Utah). By the time Young died in 1877, Salt Lake City had 140,000 inhabitants.

Several religious groups founded in Europe sought refuge from persecution in the western United States and Canada, including the Mennonites, who came from Switzerland by way of the Rhineland. Their sects included the Amish of eastern Pennsylvania. Mennonite agricultural skills and industrious ways gave these immigrants an influence out of proportion to their numbers. Others came from Italy, Germany, Ireland and Eastern Europe to escape poverty, or the revolutionary social upheavals of the late 1840s. Most were family people who staked out remote land claims on the basis of the Homestead Acts, beginning in 1862, when 160 acres per resident family were offered for $1.25 an acre. This represented wealth and security beyond the dreams of most immigrants, many of whom had already experienced crowded conditions and unemployment in Eastern ports of arrival. Some newcomers from European cities found work as merchants, cooks, seamstresses, carpenters, barbers—skills they had practiced at home.

Chinese laborers imported to work on the transcontinental railroad faced low wages, long hours and active hostility from American citizens. Discriminatory federal laws barred the naturalization of Chinese immigrants, and their lack of civil rights made them vulnerable to exploitation. Chinese women on the West Coast were often pressured into prostitution, while Chinese men, who in 1877 comprised some 8 percent of California's population, furnished one-fourth of the state's day laborers—at substandard wages. It would be many years before Chinese immigrants were protected against sporadic rioting and destruction of their homes and businesses, although a few prospered in the import-export trade in Oriental goods. For them, the "promised land" they found in the American West was called the "Golden Mountain."

Opposite: Mormon families sent out from Utah to claim land in Arizona pose in front of a "dog trot" log cabin – twin structures with a wagon run between them. Settlements like this one, near Snowflake, were made to win converts and provide support to Mormons far from Salt Lake City.

A SPIRITUAL ODYSSEY

Opposite: Twelve thousand Mormons begin their exodus from Nauvoo, Illinois, in February 1846, after their prophet, Joseph Smith, was killed by an angry mob opposed to Mormon teachings on polygamy. *Right:* Mormon converts from England, Wales and Scandinavia made their way overland to Deseret (Utah) pulling 500-pound handcarts, as seen in this woodcut from the 1850s. "Zion's Express" was one of the slogans that sustained their enthusiasm. *Below:* A Mormon wagon train fords the South Platte River, Nebraska, in 1866.

HOMESTEADS IN
THE PROMISED LAND

Left: Mormon women and children pose in front of a dairy building in their Arizona community, which would become known as Mormon Lake. *Opposite:* "The Saints" were rarely at rest, apart from special occasions like this visit by photographer Ben Wittick. Known for their industrious ways, they made the desert bloom with irrigation systems, shared resources and intensive cultivation of land that no one else wanted.

POLYGAMY—THEORY AND PRACTICE

Opposite: A Mormon patriarch with his six wives. Men who had a place in the church hierarchy and could afford to support large families were encouraged to form plural marriages—a major source of anti-Mormon prejudice, until the practice was outlawed by Congress. *Right:* Brigham Young, president of the Mormon Church and first governor of Utah Territory, was lampooned in this portrait featuring his "cabinet" of thirty-six wives. In fact, he had twenty-seven wives and fifty-seven children, based on Joseph Smith's injunction to restore the Biblical practice of polygamy. The Mormons did not forbid plural marriages until 1890. *Below:* An engraving of the three wives of a pioneer to the State of Deseret.

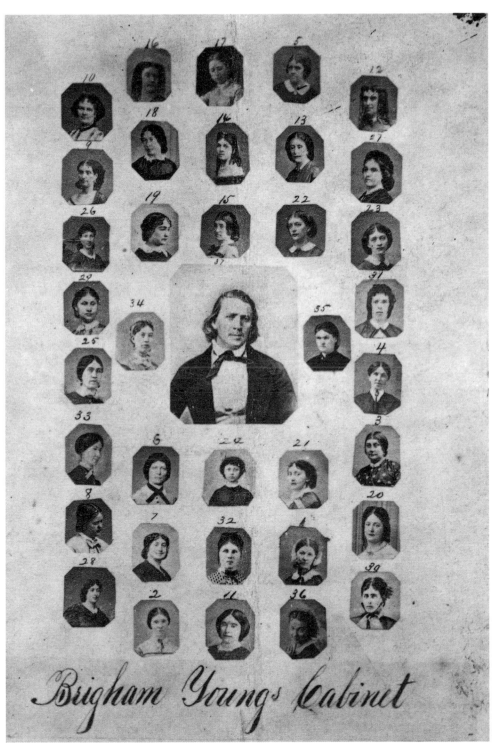

Brigham Young's Cabinet

THE NEW ZION

Below: The famous Mormon Tabernacle in Salt Lake City, with its 3,000-pipe organ decorated for Independence Day, 1880. Built in 1867, the Tabernacle stands on Temple Square and has a 250-foot self-supporting oval dome. It has a capacity of more than 12,000 people. *Opposite:* Brigham Young's Salt Lake City residence in 1866, almost twenty years after Mormon settlement. Both a visionary and a pragmatist, Young brought the fledgling community to self-sufficiency before his death in 1877.

OLD WORLD TO NEW

Above: Prosperity has proved elusive for this Italian family transplanted to New Mexico. *Opposite:* Immigrants from Italy pose in their flourishing barbershop, the Battaglia, in Pueblo, Colorado. *Top right:* Russian immigrants to Saskatchewan, lacking draft animals, harness themselves together to plow their land. *Right:* A German woman's face shows the strain of continuous childbearing in this studio portrait.

RITES OF PASSAGE

Opposite: A traditional Slovac wedding unites the families of immigrants John Sajbel and Anna Rajz for their new life in the West. *Below:* The hard-working Miketa clan brings an Eastern European flavor to their christening celebration in the Colorado Rockies.

"GOLDEN MOUNTAIN"

Chinese immigrants to the West Coast suffered exploitation, racism and violence as they sought to establish a foothold. They were confined to menial jobs like laundering (above) and railroad building (left), where their willingness to work long hours for low pay gave rise to the derogatory term "coolie wages." Mob violence broke out in San Francisco, where Chinese "wash houses" were destroyed, and twenty-two Chinese were killed in Los Angeles rioting by other laborers in October 1871.

Right: Some enterprising merchants, like Vee Wing of Pike's Peak, Colorado, became purveyors of imported luxury goods to successful miners, bankers and others who found the fortunes they had sought in the West.
Below: Many Chinese girls were pressed into prostitution in Western brothels, or sold themselves to survive when promised work or marriages failed to materialize after they crossed the Pacific.

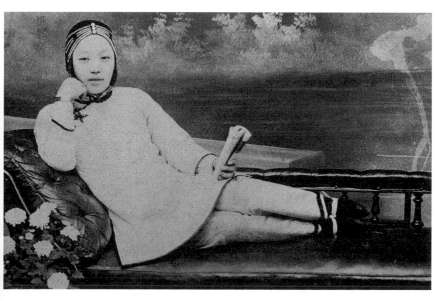

O Pioneers!

By 1840 the U.S. population stood at only 17,069,453, and the geographic center of the nation's population was just south of present-day Clarksburg, West Virginia. These figures give some idea of the immensity of the wilderness traveled and settled by the pioneers. Whether they struck new roots in the Southwest, the Great Plains, or the rugged region between the Rockies and the Sierras, they faced common problems in securing shelter, food, livestock, tools and household furnishings.

Most families brought only a few essentials on the long trek west—rifles and hunting knives, axes, corn meal, iron kettles, seeds and draft animals. The most fortunate had a cow for milk and breeding. New furniture, clothes and utensils were made on the spot, with few tools and much inventiveness, from whatever materials were available.

Plains dugouts and sod houses offered good protection from the cold, but their turf roofs, supported by poles, leaked torrents of muddy water in wet weather. The adobe coating on Southwestern shelters of sun-dried brick had to be constantly renewed for weatherproofing. Where wood was available, log cabins made sturdy dwellings for people and livestock, if the cracks were well chinked with moss or clay. Some of the techniques for fashioning shelter from the unfamiliar materials the settlers found were adapted from local Native American methods. Most pioneer houses were quite dark in the winter, when windows were covered with animal skins or oiled paper in the absence of glass.

Of necessity, frontier children learned many skills that made them contributors to the family's welfare. They fed poultry, collected eggs, milked cows and cleaned out stalls. Nearby woods and fields yielded nuts and berries, along with such useful herbs as balsam, catnip, pennyroyal and sage, which were brought under cultivation to vary the staples of corn, squash, potatoes and cabbage. Boys hunted and dressed game, prepared animal skins and furs for use as clothing and bedding, plowed, planted and weeded. Girls were taught spinning, knitting, weaving, candle- and soapmaking, and how to preserve foods, as well as participating in their share of the farm work.

Ranching became important from the Rio Grande to Oregon when the railroads provided Eastern markets for livestock. Free-range stock raising brought skills learned from the Mexican *vaqueros*—roping, branding, roundups, rodeos and trail drives. The cowboy and cowgirl rode into American history.

Frontier hospitality was legendary. Strangers were never refused food and lodging. The expression "the latchstring is always out" originated with the log cabin, where a deerskin latchstring secured the door at night but hung outside by day, so that anyone could lift the latch and walk in. Visits from traders and other travelers brought welcome news and sociability. Popular get-togethers included husking bees, house and barn raisings, weddings, quilting parties and log-rollings. A pervasive spirit of co-operation and fellowship did much to alleviate the isolation, hardships and dangers of frontier life.

Opposite: *A pioneer mother and child in a wheatfield near Newcastle, Wyoming, in a photograph that has become an emblem of the frontier experience.*

STAKING THEIR CLAIMS

Left: Raising a log cabin in the mountainous Idaho Territory, where wood for building was plentiful and a house-raising was a neighborhood affair—for those, at least, who had the benefit of neighbors. *Opposite:* The Old Simonson Ranch on Pumpkin Creek, Montana, combining sod-roofed log cabins and a frame shed, a later addition. *Below:* A rudimentary tent and shack hold down a family's claim to a lot in the future town of Guthrie, Oklahoma, after the former Indian Territory was opened to Anglo settlement.

SOME PLACE LIKE HOME

Above: John Curry and his wife at their Custer
County, Nebraska, homestead in 1886. Proud
possessions include a sturdy team of horses, several
working dogs, a rocking chair and a birdcage. *Opposite:*
A family portrait of the Randings of Nebraska and
their livestock in front of—and on top of—their sod
dugout on the Great Plains.

ROOM TO GROW

Opposite: A substantial sod house providing relatively comfortable shelter for several generations, graced by glass windows and a framed roof, photographed in 1887. *Right:* The Barnes family faces a problem common to Nebraska pioneers: their sod roof has collapsed under heavy rains. This windowless dwelling would be extremely dark and stuffy during the winter months.

FARMING THE LONE PRAIRIE

Opposite: Cornfields surround this Great Plains homestead, cultivated by the steel plow that made it possible to farm the deep-rooted grasslands. A large corn crib adjoins the house, with its unusual hipped roof. *Below:* Prairie dwellers had to dig deep wells to provide essential water for themselves and their livestock.

THE DAILY ROUND

Careful husbandry soon increased the pioneers' supply of livestock, providing needed milk, meat and eggs as well as draft animals. *Opposite, top:* The Wolverton family farm in Pondera County, Montana, where the Valier Irrigation Project allowed for diversified agriculture. *Opposite, below:* Colorado ranchers take care of their poultry. Aside from the indispensable hens, geese were raised to provide feathers for bedding. At right, a promising colt is fed by hand. *Below:* Milking was a laborious, twice-daily chore, but it often provided extra income from the sale of milk and butter for those who produced a surplus of milk.

BRINGING IN THE *SHEAVES*

Opposite: Prairie wheat farming would be
revolutionized by Cyrus McCormick's invention of the
mechanical reaper in 1831. It was soon followed by
labor-saving machines for mowing and threshing.
Below: Harvesting remained hard, hot work despite
the improvements in agricultural technology made
by the turn of the century.

TEAM EFFORTS

Harvesting brought neighbors together, not only to work, but to exchange news, forecast the weather and enjoy the fruits of their labor. *Left:* Three Iowa women and a boy pose with shocks of grain. *Opposite:* Hard work notwithstanding, apple-picking was a popular activity, which was followed by sorting, cidermaking and storage in root cellars for winter use. Pacific Northwestern orchards would become especially notable for the quality of their fruit.

SOAP AND WATER

The simple necessities for basic hygiene and laundering were not available to isolated homesteaders without a good deal of work. When water was scarce, bathing and laundry were kept to a minimum and the precious fluid was recycled carefully. *Opposite: S*oapmaking was a labor-intensive process that involved boiling animal fat with an alkaline substance like wood ash, then cooling the mixture in a crude press until it solidified into bars. *Right:* A vigorous Nebraska pioneer, Mrs. Ted Pope, shows rare enthusiasm for the task of pumping well water on the Great Plains.

INGENUITY AT WORK

Several inventions helped lighten the load on washday, including (above) a makeshift hand-operated, rocker-type washing machine, and (right) the newfangled paddle washer and hand-cranked wringer that came in with the twentieth century. *Opposite:* Rancher Homer T. Goodell of Philbrook, Nebraska, shows off the engine he rigged up to power his wife Ruby's old-fashioned washing machine.

WOMAN'S WORK

Overleaf: Woman's work on the frontier was almost
anything that needed doing, including (from left) sawing
firewood; keeping things clean without indoor plumbing;
tending beehives; and preparing big meals for hungry
"hands" and family.

THE CATTLE KINGDOM

Left: At a round-up on the Sherman Ranch in Genesee, Kansas, a cowboy readies his lasso for the signal to close in on the herd. Kansas was a major railhead for cattle shipment, centered around Abilene, Kansas City and Dodge City. *Opposite:* Cowgirls at Oklahoma's 101 Ranch relied on the speed and strength of their wiry cattle ponies, many of which were wild mustangs captured and trained to work the livestock herds.

FAMILY ENTERPRISES

Opposite: The Crabtrees of Arizona Territory hunted and trapped with their hounds. The burros served both as mounts and pack animals. Docile and hard-working, they were descended from donkeys introduced by the Spanish some 300 years earlier. *Below:* The Becker sisters pitch in to brand a calf on their ranch in Colorado's San Luis Valley. Unmarked free-ranging stock was easily appropriated by rustlers.

SCENE AT A SAN LOU'S VALLY CATTLE RANCH

O T DAVIS Photo No 236

KEEPING THE TABLE SUPPLIED

Left: Where anthracite coal was available, it was used to fire large ovens—often communal—for breadmaking. Other fuels included wood and kerosene. Ovens and smokehouses were usually separate from the main house to reduce the risk of fire. *Opposite:* An elderly woman peels a bountiful crop of peaches for preserving in front of the family smokehouse.

DOING THEIR PART
Pioneer children took pride in their contributions to the family welfare, as seen at local fairs and livestock shows. *Opposite:* A little girl poses with a mammoth prize-winning squash at Nebraska's Custer County Fair. *Right:* Puzzled turkeys are hitched up to the produce wagon by a young entrepreneur in Wisconsin.

Our Town

The American frontier experience fostered traits that would become identified with the national character, from "Yankee ingenuity" to Missouri's "Show Me" attitude and the cowboy's "horse sense." American society was continuously re-created as people moved farther west for adventure, opportunity and what one pioneer called simply "a strong bent of their spirits for change"; new immigrants, too, brought diverse customs and traditions from around the world. All of these qualities marked the new communities that sprang up once survival was no longer in the balance.

Gradually, the brawling, wide-open mining and cattle towns grew tamer under the influence of ad hoc lawmen and increasing numbers of women. Disappointed Forty-Niners took up farming or ranching and started families. Rough frontier forts acquired some polish from their officers' wives, and "mail-order brides" brought flower seeds and fashionable hats from the East Coast. Once settled, women began to undertake new roles and took the lead in creating a community life. Frontier society became more stratified; libraries and literary societies were organized to meet the growing need for culture, while issues like temperance and morality came to the fore.

The itinerant schoolmaster who "boarded out" with local families was eventually replaced by small-town schools with permanent teachers. And frontier children who had been scarcely literate when school kept—if at all—for three months of the year reluctantly donned shoes and attended classes with some regularity. Their schools were often of the one-room variety; books and paper were in short supply, but they learned the basics of arithmetic, grammar and composition. Elocution contests and poetry readings were attended by proud parents, and musical recitals became popular.

New churches of various denominations brought people together for worship. Community-wide church socials enhanced the growth of religious tolerance among different sects—although Roman Catholics, Jews and "foreigners" still had to make their way among the Protestant majority. As in small towns everywhere, gossip and criticism were prevalent, but they were tempered by the traditions of neighborliness and concern for the common good.

Law and order began to replace the "frontier justice" of what was long called the Wild West, with its outlaws, vigilantes, livestock rustlers, deputy sheriffs and hanging judges like Roy Bean—known in Texas as "law west of the Pecos." Muddy Main Streets were paved, and board sidewalks installed. Merchants offered a wider variety of goods, especially after completion of the transcontinental railroad in 1869. Frontier towns might now display haberdashery and millinery along with hardware, flour, calico and farm supplies. Sewing circles, charitable organizations—even theaters, opera houses and atheneums—evolved to meet the changing needs of frontier society. But each new community retained the imprint of its origins: individualism, enterprise and an abiding faith in both Providence and democracy.

Opposite: San Francisco's Seven Mile House exemplified the masculine preserve known as the saloon, as seen in this photograph from the 1860s. At this time, San Francisco and Denver were the two largest cities west of the Mississippi.

MAIN-STREET BUSINESSES

Below: Apparently, residents of Lane County, Oregon, saw nothing alarming in the proximity of the local hospital to the undertaker's establishment downstairs! In this multi-purpose arrangement, the same carpenters produced both furniture and coffins for the local community. *Opposite:* By 1913 Iowa City, Iowa, boasted an elegant millinery shop run by the Adams sisters, complete with ornate mirrors and glass display cases for the latest in fashionable hats and trimmings.

TOWN SCHOOLS GET HIGHER MARKS

Overleaf: By the 1890s, education was a high priority in thriving Western communities like Hecla, Montana (page 104), where Miss Blanche Lamont posed at her board-and-batten schoolhouse with some thirty pupils of varying ages and sizes. Iowa's Bear Creek Township School (page 105) stressed the virtues of piety and patriotism along with geography, history and the basic "three R's."

VOLATILE ISSUES

In the emerging communities of the West, there were few pre-existing rules and traditions, and social issues were approached with greater openness. *Left:* Denver women achieved the vote by popular referendum in 1893, twenty-four years after the progressive Wyoming Territory enfranchised its women. *Opposite:* Prominent Western activists for women's rights included the formidable Carry Nation (far right), who waged her crusade for temperance with a hatchet wielded against the bottles and glassware of luxurious saloons like the Senate Bar of Topeka, Kansas. Many deplored her tactics, but respected her objective—eliminating the suffering caused to women and children by alcoholic husbands and fathers.

ON THE WILD SIDE

Prostitution on the frontier took various forms, from women who sold their favors to itinerant cowboys and miners in bawdy houses like the one below, to "companions" hired out for the night by madams who purveyed women to the patrons of Colorado's Cripple Creek Saloon (opposite) and similar watering holes. If they were fortunate, such women could save enough to leave town and resurface elsewhere as respectable widows eligible for remarriage.

NEW AMENITIES AND ENTERTAINMENTS

By the turn of the century, families who had prospered in the West could entertain lavishly, like the party at left, captured by an ingenious photographer. New communities imbued with the spirit of the frontier would continue to spring up, shaped by the ideals and principles that had fueled the great westward migration.

INDEX

Page references that appear in **boldface** refer to illustrations.

Abilene, Kans. 8, 92
Acoma Pueblo 13
Adams family 102, **103**
adobe construction 8, **12**, 13, **14**, 15, **15**, **20**, **21**, 22, 71,
African Americans 9, **32**, 33, **48**, 48, 50, 51, **51**, **52**, 53
Alaska 43
Allegheny Mountains 7
American River, Calif. 8
Anadarko, Okla. **25**, 25
Anasazi 13, 15
Anglo settlement 7, 8, 18, 72
Apache 8, **25**, 25
Arapahoe **17**
Armitage, Susan 7
Austin, Stephen 7

Barnes family **77**, 77
Bean, Roy 101
Becker family **95**, 95
Bell, Laura **48**, 48
Biffle, Primus 50, 51
"Big Bonanza" 33
Big Timber, Kans. 29
Boone, Daniel 7
British Columbia 25, 43
Brown, Clara 51, **51**

Canadian subarctic 18
candlemaking 71
Canyon de Chelly, Ariz. **15**
Cattle Kingdom 8, 92
Cheyenne, Wy. 9
Chinese immigrants 11, 55, **68**, 68, 69, **69**

Chloride, N.M. 28, **29**
Church of Jesus Christ of Latter- Day Saints see Mormons
churches 22, **23**, 101
Civil War 9, 13, 31, 33
Conestoga wagon 33, **38**
Cooper, James Fenimore 7
Cowboys Gang 29
cowboys/cowgirls 8, 11, **92**, 92, **93**
Crabtree family **94**, 95
Cripple Creek, Colo. **108**
Cumberland Gap 7
Curry family **74**, 74
Curtis, Edward S. 18
Custer County (Neb.) Fair **98**, 99
Custer, George A. 13, **29**, 29

Deadwood, S.D. 37
Denver, Colo. 9, 101, 106, **107**
Deseret 55, 57, 61
Dodge City, Kans. 8, 92
dugouts 7, 71, 74, **75**
Dyea River 46, **47**

education 9, **10**, 11, 24, **25**, 25, 101, **103**, **104**, 105
Emigrant, The 40
European immigrants 55, 57, **57**, **64**, 65, **66**, **67**, 67

Forty-Niners 101 see also gold rush
French-Candians 13
Frontier Thesis 7, 33
Ft. McDowell (Ariz.) **29**, 29
Ft. Pierre (S.D.) 40
Ft. Wingate (N.M.) **30**, 31

ghost towns 9
gold rush: California 8, **9**, 33, **44**, 45; Klondike 9, **42**, **43**, 43, 46, **47**
Goldhill, Nev. 8
Goodell family 88, **89**
Great Basin 9, 55
Great Plains 7, 8, 13, **16**, **17**, **78**, **79**
Green, Annie 11
Gulf of California 13
Guthrie, Okla. 72

hacienda 22, **22**
Hannah, Edward 50, **51**
Harbor, Sybil 51, **51**
Harte, Bret 46
harvesting 83, **84**, 84
Hispanic families 13, 22, **22**, 23
Hohman family **11**
Homestead Acts 55
Hopi 15, **15**
horno **21**, 21
household tasks 9, **21**, 71, **79**, 81, **81**, 86, **87**, 88, **88**, 89, **89**, **90–91**, 96, **96**, **97**

Idaho Territory **72**, 72
Indian Territory 17, 48, **72**, 72
Inuit **18**
Iowa City, Ia. 102, **103**

Jenkins, Mrs. George 55, **55**
Johnson, William 48, **48**
Josephy, Alvin M., Jr. 7

Kansas City, Kans. 92
Kiowa **17**, 17
Klondike, the 9, **42**, **43**, 43, 46, **47**

Lane County, Ore. 102, **102**
"law and order" 26, **26**, 101
Leadville, Colo. 8
Lee, Jason 7
log cabins 54, 55, 58, 59, 71, **72**, **73**, **74**, 74
Los Angeles, Calif. 68

"mail-order brides" 9, 101
McCormick, Cyrus 83
Melton, Ira **48**, 48
Mennonites 55
Mesa Verde, Colo. 13
Mexican War 13
Mexicans 8, **22**, 22, 23
Mexico 8, 13, 22, 29
military posts **28**, **29**, **30**, **31**, 31, 101
mining towns 7, 8–9, 33, **44**, 45, **45**, 46, **47**
missionaries 13, **24**, 25, **25**
Mississippi River 7, 33, 40, 48
Missouri River 40, **41**
mixed (interethnic) marriages 11, 13, **26**, 26
Mora Valley, N.M. 22
Mormon Lake, Ariz. **58**, 58
Mormons 6, 7, 9, **54**, 55, 56, **57**, 57, **58**, 58, 59, **60**, 61, 61–62
Mormon Tabernacle **62**, 62
Mountain men 7, **26**, **27**
music halls 11, 46

Nation, Carry 106, **107**
Native American displacement 8
Nauvoo, Ill. 55, 56, **57**
Navajo country 38, **39**
Needles Rock, Utah **6**, 7
Nevada Territory 8, 33
Newcastle, Wy. **70**, 71

Ninth Cavalry **30**, **31**, 31

Oglala Sioux **17**
Ohio River 40
Ojibwa 18, **19**
Omaha, Neb. 9
Oregon Trail 33
"oxbow" route 37

Piegan **16**, 17
Pike's Peak, Colo. **45**, **69**, 69
polygamy 55, 57, **60**, 61, **61**
Pope, Mrs.Ted **87**
Prairie Schooner see Conestoga wagon; wagon trains
prospectors 8, **9**, **42**, **43**, 43, 44, **45**
prostitution 11, 55, **69**, 69, **108**, **109**
Pueblo peoples 8, **12**, 13, **15**, 15
Pueblo, Colo. 65

saloons **100**, 101, 106, **108**, **109**
Salt Lake City, Ut. 9, 55, **62**, 63
San Francisco, Calif. 9, **68**, 101
San Ildefonso Pueblo 15
Sand Hills, Neb. 51, **51**
Santa Fe, N.M. 9, **22**, 22, 31
Santa Fe Trail 33
Saskatchewan, Can. **65**, 65
schools 9, **10**, 101, **103**, **104**, 105
Seminoles **25**, 25
Seventh Cavalry **29**, 29
Seymour, Elizabeth 51, **51**
Shipaulovi, Ariz. 15
Shores family **32**, 33

Sierra Nevada 8
Silverton, Colo. 8
Smith, Jedediah 7
Smith, Joseph 55, 57, 61
Snowflake, Ariz. 54, 63
soapmaking 71, 86, **87**
sod houses 7, **11**, **32**, 48, 71, **74**, **75**, **76**, **77**, **78**, **79**
spinning 51, 71
Speese family 48, **49**
St. Louis, Mo. 33
stagecoaches 33, **36**, 37
Summer family 48, **49**

temperance movement 9, 101, 106, **107**
Tenth Cavalry **28**, 29
threshing 82, **83**, 83
Turner, Frederick Jackson 7, 33

Union Pacific Railroad 33

Valier (Mont.) Irrigation Project 81
vaqueros 8, 71
Virginia City, Nev. 33

wagon trains 6, **7**, 7, 8, **8**, 33, **34**, **35**, 35, **37**, 37, **56**, **57**, 57
weaving 71
Weber River, Utah 38, **39**
well water 7, **22**, **79**, 79, 87
Wild West shows 7
Wilderness Road 7
Wittick, Benjamin 31, 58
Wolverton family **80**, 81
woman suffrage 9, **106**, 106

Young, Brigham 55, **61**, 61, 62
Yukon Territory **47**, 47

BIBILIOGRAPHY

Bowman, John S., ed. *The World Almanac of the American West*. N.Y.: Pharos Books, 1986.

Daniels, George G. *The Spanish West*, The Old West series. N.Y.: Time-Life Books, 1976.

Grafton, John. *The American West in the Nineteenth Century*. N.Y.: Dover Publications, 1992.

Katz, William Loren. *The Black West*. N.Y.: Simon & Schuster, 1996.

Ketchum, Richard M., ed. *The American Heritage Book of the Pioneer Spirit*. N.Y.: Crown Publishers, 1994.

Lawliss, Chuck. *The Old West Sourcebook: A Traveler's' Guide*. N.Y.: Crown Publishers, 1994.

McLoughlin, Denis. *Wild and Woolly: An Encyclopedia of the Old West*. N.Y.: Barnes & Noble Books, 1995.

Newark, Peter, and Robin May. *The Old West: An Illustrated History of Cowboys and Indians*. Greenwich, Conn.: Bison Books, 1984.

Peavy, Linda, and Ursula Smith. *Pioneer Women: The Lives of Women on the Frontier*. Rowayton, Conn.: Saraband, 1996.

Prescott, Jerome, ed. *The Unspoiled West: The Western Landscape as Seen by Its Greatest Photographers*. N.Y.: Smithmark, 1994.

Steer, Diana. *Native American Women*. N.Y.: Barnes and Noble, 1996.

Thomas, David Hurst. *The Native Americans: An Illustrated History*. Atlanta: Turner Publishing, 1993.

Walker, Steven L. *The Southwest: A Pictorial History of the Land and the People*. Scottsdale, Ariz.: Camelback/Canyonlands, 1993.

ACKNOWLEDGEMENTS

The publisher would like to thank Robin Langley Sommer, Sara Hunt, Charles J. Ziga, Nicola J. Gillies and Wendy Ciaccia Eurell for their assistance in the preparation of this book, as well as the following individuals and institutions for their kind permission to reproduce the photographs on the pages listed below:

Archives Division—Texas State Library: 51L (1963/283-53); **Idaho State Historical Society**: 27 (#65.R8.J8), 44 (#730882), 72T (60-72-43), 88L (#72-193.9); **Kansas State Historical Society**: 29L, 29TL, 52, 53TR; **Lane County Historical Museum**: 86, 102; **Library of Congress, Prints and Photographs Division**: 5, 9, 14, 15BL, 15R, 16, 18BL, 18BR, 25L & R, 34, 36, 37, 40, 42I, 43, 44I, 45L, 46 (both), 47 (both), 49TR, 51TC & R, 56, 57T, 60, 61 (both), 68 (both), 72B, 76, 79, 80B, 81, 83, 85, 93, 95, 96, 97, 99, 100, 104, 106, 107, 109; **Local History Collection, Pike's Peak Library District**: 45L, 69R, 91L; **Montana Historical Society, Helena**: 73, 80T, 89, 90R, 108; **Museum of New Mexico**: 8 (I. Carbutt, # 65054), 15TL (T. Harmon Parkhurst, #5144), 20 (Ed Andrews, # 71218), 21 (Christian G. Kaadt, # 69106), 22T (#22468), 22B (T. Harmon Parkhurst, # 15152), 28 (Henry A. Schmidt, # 58556), 30 (#98374), 31 (Ben Wittick, # 50887), 38T (T. Harmon Parkhurst, # 8191), 39T (#59590), 39B (Ben Wittick, # 3083), 54 (# 15615), 57B (Charles R. Savage, # 65097), 59 (Ben Wittick, # 15682); **National Archives of Canada**: 18TL, 19, 24, 42B, 65TR; **National Archives (U.S)**: 23, 58, 92, 94; **Nebraska State Historical Society**: 2, 6, 11, 38B, 49B, 50R, 53BR, 62, 63, 74, 75, 77, 78, 98; **Peter Palmquist Collection**: 1, 26L, 26R, 65BR, 69TL, 69BL, 110; **Pueblo Library District**: 12, 48, 50L, 51BC, 53L, 64, 65TL, 66, 67; **Sharlot Hall Museum Library/Archives, Prescott, Arizona**: 29R, 90L, 91R; **South Dakota State Historical Society**: 4, 10, 35, 41, 82; **State Historical Society of Iowa, Iowa City**: 84, 88R, 103, 105; **State Historical Society of North Dakota**: 87; **Wyoming State Museum—Division of Cultural Resources**: 17 (all), 70.